# Introduction

It is truly strange how long it takes *to get to know oneself*. I am now sixty-two years old, yet just one moment ago I realised that I *love* lightly toasted bread. Simultaneously, I also realised that I *loathe* bread when it is heavily toasted. For over sixty years, and quite unconsciously, I have been experiencing inner joy or total despair at my relationship with grilled bread.

Ludwig Wittgenstein, Cambridge, 27 April 1951

## Case Study #01: Birth Drinking

I'll never forget him coming round to our house. He banged repeatedly on the front door. He was shouting, nearly screaming: 'DAVE! DAVE!' I remember my Dad sighing heavily as he went to answer the door.

'What's up with you?'
'We've had a little girl!' His fat face was flushed bright red, he was pissed out of his mind. 'Finally Dave! We've had a little girl!'
'That's great. You'd better come in.'
As I think of it now, I can hear the nonchalance ... I can hear the distance in my Dad's voice, 'Erm ... would you like a drink?'
'I'll have a whiskey.' He stumbled through the door and into our front room.

I was watching telly, it was dark outside and I remember it as being Christmas. I'd never seen anybody that drunk before. He was SHOUTING not speaking, sweating booze.

'8lbs 2oz,' he kept saying, or something like that, something to do with weight. 'I think we're gonna call her Julie.'

'Here you go,' my Dad handed him a whiskey. 'Well. Congratulations.'

After a few years, it  was clear that Julie wasn't playing with a full deck ... I mean, she wasn't the brightest lamp in our street. He became increasingly unlikable. And he was extremely unlikable in the first place, so it took no small effort on his part to become really unlikable. Julie had a baby herself, while still in her mid-teens. To the best of my knowledge, he is still drinking all day, every day. Still celebrating his miraculous reproduction.*

*He tried to start a fight with me once, many years ago. His gigantic head was purple with booze and rage. It was in the Percy Arms, our local pub. I told him to *fuck off*. I never really liked him, neither did my Dad. Two decades later (in fact only yesterday), I realised that he was probably drunk before Julie was born, I realised that he'd always been drunk.[†]

† 10/04/08 – I just got a text message saying that he died today, cirrhocis of the liver.

## Case Study #02: Alone Again

My stereo finally broke today. It'd been going wrong for ages, the left speaker
working and the right not, then vice versa. We've been through a lot together, I
mean *really*. We've been in love since 1998. I bought it to console myself when
Lucy left me. I spent all the money I had on it. It's been my best friend for ten
years. We've done so much together, we've lived in five different houses, we've
listened to a million white men shouting. THE TWAT BASTARD. It's like losing a Labrador. I can't believe it. All the times I've slapped it and shouted at  it
for making CDs skip. And now it's finally left me. YOU BASTARD. What am
I going to do? This always happens to me. Please come back.


**Exercise #01: Your automatic response to case study #02:**

.............................................................................................

.............................................................................................

.............................................................................................

.............................................................................................

.............................................................................................

.............................................................................................

.............................................................................................

- I shouldn't have put broken glass in that bin bag.

- Or at least I should've wrapped it up in newspaper – several sheets, then taped it up as well.

- The binman is bound to cut his hand.

- He's going to sue me. It's not the suing that I'm bothered about.

- He'll think I'm some ignorant thought-less arsehole who doesn't care about him or his hand.

- He'll probably stop taking my rubbish, and I don't blame him.

- If he won't collect my rubbish I'll end up with rats in my garden.

- I'm trying to sell my house.

- How will I ever sell my house with rats running about?

- It'll be my fault. It is my fault.

- I'll write to the Council and apologise.

- But, If I let them know that I'm still here, they'll start chasing me for unpaid Council tax.

- Then I'll have to pay off the three year backlog of Council tax.

- I haven't got three-and-a-half grand to pay the fucking Council tax.

- They'll send the bailiffs round. I can't let them take my computer.

- It's got all my ideas on it.

- I should start to print off all my ideas and save them in a binder.

- My printer doesn't work.

- And I don't have a CD burner.

- I should start to e-mail everyone I know … a few files each.

- The binman will think I'm some kind of arrogant yuppie who doesn't care about his health or his job.

- I should definitely write the binman a note to explain:

- 'I was in a rush, I was on my way out, I was late.'

- He won't believe me. I'll explain that I'm from working-class stock and that under different circumstances it could easily have been MY HAND that was shredded. Think about that!

- It's no use. He'll probably know that I went to college.

- I'll misspell everything and tell him that I have learning difficulties.

- I'll tell him that I didn't know that I was doing wrong.

- I'll tell him that my care worker has since explained just how VERY WRONG it was.

- He won't believe me.

- The fact that I can make objective judgements and have the capacity to rationalise and then apologise will be a clear indication of the fact that I'm not educationally sub-normal or psychotic.

- I could tell him that I'm a dangerous psychopath and that if he wants to make a big deal about ONE shredded hand then he's a total coward and if he complains to me or the Council I'll cut his shredded hand off with an axe.

- That's no use. If I say that he'll go to the police and they'll come round and arrest me. I don't want to be arrested.

- If I got sent to prison, I'd never cope. I can't go to prison.

- Jesus Christ. Mr. Big might try and make me his bitch.

- I don't exactly enjoy my freedom, but, even having a job was too much for me. I hated being told what to do. It was Hell. Prison will be at least 10,000 times worse.

- I'll wait down the street next time the binmen come. When they get to my house I'll casually walk past pretending I'm my own neighbour.

- I'll stop and chat casually to the binmen and I will ask them:

- 'Have you heard about the bloke from No.35? ... the one who leaves broken glass in his bin bag?'

- I'll tell them that No.35 killed himself in a fit of despair.

- I'll explain that No.35 lost his entire family in an explosion at a working-class factory.

- If they believe me they'll forget about the glass incident. It'll seem trivial by comparison.

- But I'll have to hide every Thursday morning when they come to collect the rubbish.

- OR: I could file a complaint about the binman.

- I could get a petition together and forge all my neighbour's signatures.

- Say that we're sick of him swearing and dropping litter everywhere. I

- could get him fired. But if I get him fired he might find out why. Then if he finds out that I'm still alive he'll probably kill me.

- If I get into a fight with the binman he'll kick the shit out of me. I'm too fat to fight. I'm a terrible fighter.

- If he did kick the shit out of me I could file a legitimate complaint against him.

- I could get HIM arrested, then HE'LL have to go to prison, then HE'LL end up being Mr. Big's bitch.

- Oh no. Then he'll become friends with hardened criminals. As they sit sewing mail bags, he'll tell them the story of how I ruined his life. I'll become a hate figure to every murderer and gangster in Wormwood Scrubs.

- Then when one of his criminal mates gets out, HE'LL KILL ME.

- But that won't be for at least a year.

- By then I should've sold my house.

- But, in the current property climate I could still be here.

- Mortgage/loan interest rates are such that I could be here for years.

- The problem with my house is that it's between price ranges.

- It's too expensive for most first time buyers but not big enough for a family.

- I have no choice. I have to get away from here. I'll have to sell quickly for a massive loss.

- But then I won't have enough money to buy another house.

- Then I'll be homeless.

## Case Study #03: Self Loathing/Exercise #02 (B)

**A.** I am not a *bad person*. I really have to remember that. I do stupid things. I'm a *stupid person*, seemingly intent on humiliating myself. God only knows why. It's like I've decided to take out an endless experiment with alcohol and misery ... on myself. What a total idiot/wanker/moron. I should've conducted my endless experiment on someone else.

## B. Is the pain so great that you have to kill yourself?

## Exercise #2A: Other Moods (complete the list)*

| MOOD LIST | | |
|---|---|---|
| Depressed | Hurt | **Other Moods:** |
| Sad | Happy | ........................ |
| Insecure | Guilty | ........................ |
| Nervous | Frightened | ........................ |
| Enraged | Panicky | ........................ |
| Anxious | Cheerful | ........................ |
| Embarrassed | Loving | ........................ |
| Proud | Ashamed | ........................ |
| Disgusted | Irritated | ........................ |
| Scared | Frustrated | ........................ |
| Angry | Disappointed | ........................ |
| Excited | Humiliated | ........................ |
| Mad | Regretful | ........................ |

* Recent research has proved that it is impossible to experience 'non-moods'. Any individual who is determinedly in a 'non-mood' is actually in a mood. They are in a *determined mood*. It is better to recognise your moods and accept them. Fighting moods or attempting a 'non-mood' is counterproductive.

## Case Study #04: Richard

Hello, I'm Richard, I'm also just nipping to the off-licence before I go into town. *I hate immigrants*. Actually, I don't. I just said it to see how it felt ... to test the notion, test the idea. Artists have to think thoughts like that to test them out, it's our job. Sometimes I go into the off-licence and imagine what it would be like to be a racist. I imagine what it would be like to smash the fucking shop to pieces and shag that bastard's daughter – God she is so fit – she's only about seventeen or fifteen, I can't tell. She talks in this horrible Cockney Jamaican patois – I don't know why. She's comes from the fucking Punjab – *actually* she's doesn't, she comes from Bethnal Green. I don't know why I said Punjab. Freud probably. It wasn't really me. I'm just testing out the possibilities of my personality. I test out the extremities of my Anglo-Saxon persona. It's my job.

Julia thinks I'm an alcoholic, but Julia's the kind of person who thinks Jackson Pollock was an alcoholic who threw a bit of paint around. I'm not an alcoholic. I just go on binges. I've tried to stop, but what's the point? I get so bored. It's because I've got a restless mind. I just can't turn off. I can't stop thinking about work. I am obsessed by my work. I am an obsessive character – everybody says so – all genius types are obsessive – we have to be – that's not true – we are geniuses because we are obsessive. That **IS** true.

'Good morning Richard!'
'Morning.'

*Bollocks*, it's the son. He's a weird one. He talks like an Oxford don and dresses like a gangsta rapper. I think he's studying economics somewhere or other, he's not usually here. I hang around where the newspapers are laid out, looking at the stupid fucking headlines 'BIG BROTHER NIKKI WAS £500 A NIGHT CALL GIRL' on *The Sun*, 'PALASTINIAN ROCKETS CAUSE CHAOS IN ISRAEL' on *The Guardian*, all that sort of stuff. Then I try and read across the headlines, seeing only the words and ignoring the papers, 'PALASTINIAN ROCKETS CAUSE CHAOS IN £500 A NIGHT CALL GIRL'. This is the sort of thing I do all day. I can't stop myself. It's an obsession. I pick up a paper, any paper. I don't care about the news, I only read the headlines. I only buy the newspaper to cover up the bottle of wine.

## Exercise #03: Do you think Richard is a racist alcoholic?

## Case Study #05: Smoking

James and Melissa Potter always used to enjoy an 'after-dinner cigarette'. Last December, having no cigarettes of her own, Melissa took her husband's last cigarette as he dozed on the sofa. When he awoke he was enraged to find he had no cigarettes left and  began beating his wife. Terrified and bleeding from the head, she fled the house. Later that night Melissa returned and set light to her husband while he slept.

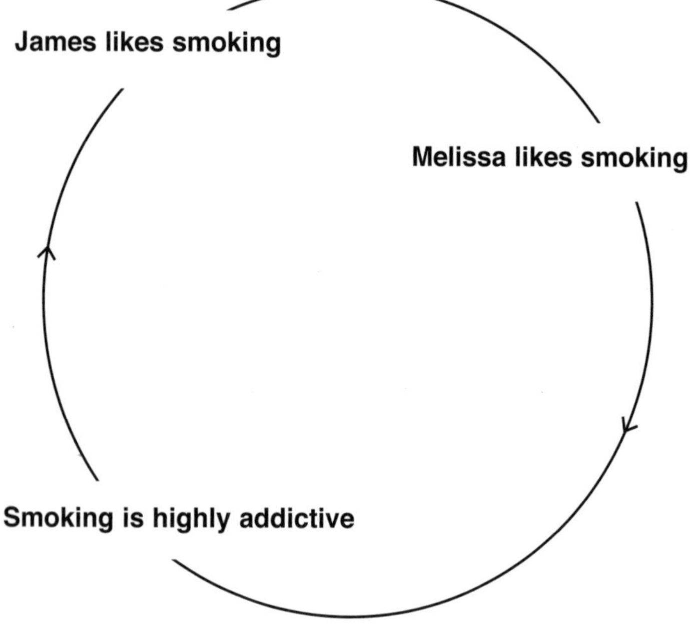


Diagram #01: Smoking

## Exercise #04: Who is to blame for unhappiness?

## Exercise #05: Consider and complete:

I don't think Helen likes me.

What's so bad about that?.........................................................................

................................................................................

................................................................................

Whenever I get close, people end up disliking me.

What does this say about me?...............................................

................................................................................

................................................................................

I'll never have a close relationship.

What does this say about me?...............................................

................................................................................

................................................................................

**I am unlikable.**

**Why?**......................................................................

..........................................................................

..........................................................................

..........................................................................

..........................................................................

..........................................................................

..........................................................................

..........................................................................

..........................................................................

..........................................................................

## Extended Case Study #01: Julian

Julian Woodcock awakens from his stupor, he doesn't dress. In his underpants he stands at the kitchen table; he never sits, not for long – he paces or fidgets, but he never really sits. He's gripped by the need to 'do' – to do something – to do *anything*. It's still dark outside. He looks out of the kitchen window, down onto the street. It's pissing it down again. Buses, cars, black cabs and a brave cyclist queue at the traffic lights outside his flat, outside PFC Clapton Hallal: London's most disgusting fried chicken take-away. Fuck this. Julian flicks on the kettle then looks in the fridge. And fuck that. There's no milk, there's no anything much. There is a half bottle of Three Hammers Strong Cider, half of a 3-litre bottle. He contemplates the idiocy of starting drinking at 7 o'clock in the morning, the sadness, the stupidity of the gesture – then he does it anyway. At least it's cold – like the weather, like the kitchen.

It doesn't take him long to get into to the idea of drinking. The first half pint is disgusting, flat and freezing. He lights a cig – excluding the one he is smoking, he still has four left – he works out the ratios. He has about four half pints of strong cider left and if he limits himself to one cigarette per glass – and if he drinks and smokes slowly – that'll last him until 8 o'clock. At 8 o'clock Ramesh across the road will be open, and although Ramesh'll quietly disapprove, Julian can buy another bottle of Three Hammers and another packet of ten Bensons. He counts out his change onto the table – £3.90 … £2 short. He panics. Shit. He really should get a cash card; he's nearly forty for God's sake. The bank will open at 9.30. He can't wait until 9.30. He has to make a decision. Cigs or booze? STOP. What is he doing? This is ridiculous. He's not even smoked the cigs or drank the booze he's got yet. Why does he have to decide now? Anyway, Ramesh might let him have the cigs or the booze on credit – so long a he shows willing to pay for one or the other, Ramesh'll surely let him have the other one on credit? Julian always pays his debts. Ramesh knows that.

The endless need to be doing something. The piles of notebooks in the corner of the living room. Julian's notebooks go back to 1988, that's twenty years. Twenty fucking years of scribble and scrawl – of often impenetrable paralytic excitement about the latest stroke of genius, the latest project, the idea that'll make him an art star, or a filmmaking star or a novelist star or a star star – he doesn't fuss about the prefix. That's almost twenty years of largely unrealised ambition. Julian sits down at the end of his scabby sofa, he puts his glass of cider between his feet and reaches into the mountain of notebooks. He picks a book, any book – Julian pulls one from the middle of the pile – a royal blue hardback studenty kind of thing, A5 and covered in gouache and ink, with a piece of a crisp packet stapled to the front of it. He recognises it instantly, it looks studenty because it is – it's even got the date inside, November 1991. Fucking hell. He reads the notes – appalled by the ambition of his younger self, he winces – then reconsiders – appalled by unfulfilled ambition in his older self, appalled and disgusted at how his older self has let his younger self down, he winces.

Looking at the cover, Julian reads aloud, 'NOTES/4 REAL'.

He tosses the notebook back on the pile, flicks the TV on and off in an instant, then goes and stands in the kitchen again. He pours another glass of Three Hammers, it tastes better than the first. It always does. Not least, he recognises, because *the pain* has begun. It could have been the flicking through the old sketchbook, it could have been the first cigarette or drink, it could have been the two-second flash of Keith Chegwin humiliating himself for a living on early morning TV. It could've been be any number of things, he neither knew nor cared, it made no difference. All Julian knew was that after he'd been awake approximately half an hour on any given morning, he wished he wasn't awake at all. He wished he could just sleep forever. Not dead. He does not wish he was dead nor would he ever contemplate killing himself. He just wished he could go to sleep and not wake up.

The burning to do something, to be creative, to be involved. Julian can never reconcile his loafing and his boozing with his ambition. It's a terrible combination – burning ambition and bone idleness. As he always does when he's at a loss as to what to do, Julian dug out his old tape recorder from under the sink, he got down his portable Aiwa record player from the top of the bedroom wardrobe. He blew the dust off the suitcase shaped record player. He could still see the photograph of it in Littlewoods catalogue now, a young girl in a party frock smiling at the camera as she demonstrated how you could carry the record player like a suitcase. The Best Christmas Present Ever, a breakthrough in technology, the Aiwa mobile suitcase/record player, he'd had it since he was nine.

Julian sat at the kitchen table – check – have I got everything? Cigs, glass, Three Hammers bottle, ashtray, mini-microphone, record player – plugged in, check – tape recorder, plugged in, check, brand new Sony 60 minute tape, 7" record box? It's near the TV in the corner. He got the record box and opened it on the table; he hadn't bought a 7" record for years. The box was half full with old Madness records and random ex-Jukebox rubbish – every single had JULIAN WOODCOCK CLASS 4 written carefully on the reverse of it's cover.

Leaning over the tape recorder, the microphone in one hand, he keyed up a record and left the needle dangling over the scratched single on the record player. He stiffened his back, then pressed RECORD on the tape recorder. He held the microphone close to his face and took a deep breath. His eyes widened and his face contorted into a manic wraparound grin ... then he announced:

'GOOD MORNING OUT THERE IN RADIO LAND!!! This is the big one – The Hairy Croissant! – it's me kids! – BARRY LEE TRAVERS!!! Welcome to Global FM!'

There's a quick burst of sub-Beatles sound, an awful piece of proto-remixing by early 80s pop disasters Stars On 45: The BLT theme tune.

'Well here we go then folks ... Here I am BARRY LEE TRAVERS ... THE MIGHTY BLT! ... and ... it's ... time for another My Top Ten ... and with me in the studio today is The Man! The Legend! The Maverick! The Genius! – yes folks – it's Julian Woodcock. GOOOOD MORNIIIING JULIAAAAAN! CAN YOU BELIEVE IT RADIO PEEPS? J.W. IS HERE IN THE STUDIO!'

Julian drops the insane grin and reverts to back to himself, or rather a version of himself, a cool, cross-legged reluctant interviewee version of himself. He leans back from the microphone, lights a cigarette and in his best David Bowie voice, whispers, 'Hi Barry.' He then launches into a self-interview with two of his favourite alter egos:  Barry Lee Travers (Popular DJ) and Julian Woodcock (Success).

BLT: Well listeners – WHAT A COUP!! You may be familiar with Julian's work – but not the man himself … so might I say, on behalf of us all … it's a privilege, NO! AN  HONOUR! … to have you here in the studio. You usually shun publicity, don't you Julian?

JW: Normally, yes.

BLT: For those of you who don't know – Julian is the leading *enfant terrible* of his generation – a *mercurial* talent. Right?

JW: Mmm. Yeah … well, some people say so.

BLT: Anyway, enough from me, let's get on with the show … I'm sure we'd all love to hear just what kind of music inspires this young man's mind. Am I right? YES YOU ARE BARRY! I HEAR YOU CRY!  Seriously though – let's get on with it … Ready Julian?

JW: Ready when you are.

BLT: Julian, welcome to the studio.

JW: Thanks, Barry. It's great to be here.

BLT: I don't want to ponder too long over your background … I'd like to crack on with the music, but for the uninitiated among us … could YOU ponder over your background?

JW: Well … where do I begin?

BLT: Why don't you tell us about your latest project?

JW: Alright. Well, it's a major political piece. Kind of *Roots* meets *Cathy Come Home* … a kind of, one-man-war against racial and social inequality  … possibly my most accomplished piece to date. I shot it over two years … it's a film. And I'm hoping it's going to make a major splash at this year's London Film Festival. I'm reluctant to tell you more Barry … sorry. I like to keep a certain mystique about my work … at least until it's been released … I hope your listeners will understand.

BLT: We all understand Julian … you don't want your work to be pre-judged … am I right?

JW: Exactly.

BLT: So, come on. What's your first record? What's at number ten?

JW: Well. This is an old favourite … I don't want to lapse into cliché … but it's been so difficult to choose ten records … and putting them in order was even more difficult. Anyway, number ten is 'The Classical' by Manc-garage legends … The Fall.


Barry cues the record, it plays, then he fades it out.


BLT: BRILLIANT! The mighty mighty brilliant Fall! Great choice. Let's keep the vibe going Julian … moving quickly on to number nine …

JW: OK. But, if I could just say a little bit more about my latest project first?

BLT: Please do MATEY!

JW: Well … I'm hoping that this may be my first piece to actually make it on to TV …

BLT: WHAT? OUTRAGEOUS! You've never had a filmic piece shown on TV? That's SCANDALOUS!

JW: Well, I admit, it is pretty shocking. But you know what television is like … prescribed formats, market research, moronic reality shows … that fucking *cunt* Jeremy Kyle.

BLT: Sorry mate … no swearing on Global FM!

JW: Sorry. Yeah … anyway … my latest project … it deals with some serious social issues … questions of ethnicity in regards to employment … y'know? How the fat cats stay fat cats by keeping the working classes and the ethnic minorities out of the education system … particularly the higher education system … that seriously angers me … It really pisses me off …

BLT: SORRY MATE! … that's your second warning! They operate a three strikes and you're out rule here BUDDY! One more swear word and they'll take us off air … sorry mate … but please tone it down. No swearing.

JW: OK. Sorry … here's the next track then. You ready Barry? At number nine it's … well, what to my mind, is one of the greatest protest records ever made and it's a beautiful song too. One that was very important to me as a teenager … and the band are from my native Yorkshire, something I'm very proud of … they were my whole life for so long. They meant so much …

they're so underrated, anyway I'll let them speak for themselves. This is 'Kick Over the Statues' by The Redskins.

The record starts abruptly with a jump of the needle, plays, and then fades out.

BLT: Another fantastic choice. The Red Red Redskins! ... probably THE most political band of the last twenty years. Right Ju?! YEAH? Would you agree?!
JW: That's right. They were a magical band. I remember when I was growing up, I was 14 or 15 at the height of the 1984 Miner's Strike ... surrounded by poverty. It was so ... *authentic* ... and The Redskins were so important then. Not quite a lone voice amongst the dross ... but certainly, to me at least, a hugely important voice ... I think it was probably The Redskins that politicised me ... you know?
BLT: I do indeed. They didn't get much airplay here at Global I'm afraid ... due to management instigated broadcast policies, particularly throughout the miners strike, but I certainly quite liked them.
JW: What do you mean?
BLT: Well ... as much as I liked them. I wasn't allowed to play them. BIG BOSS HE SAY NO! Management gave me an ultimatum ... playing the likes of The Redskins ... at that time, it was seen to be flying The Red Flag in the face of government sponsorship. The Thatcher government heavily supported this station ... and me playing Redskins songs? Forget it MATEY! It would have been tantamount to treason ... I'd have lost my job.
JW: And what about the thousands of miners in the industrialised North, Midlands and Wales that lost their jobs?
BLT: Well, not my *problemo* really, mate! I mean, I liked the band and I believe in a kind of socialism, but ... well, you've got to look after *numero uno*! Right?
JW: YOU LOUSY HYPOCRITE BARRY. I CAN'T BELIEVE WHAT I JUST HEARD. YOU FUCKING PSEUDO LIBERAL BASTARD TRAITOR! I DON'T BELIEVE THIS.
BLT: That's it! You've blown it ... sorry listeners ... within thirty seconds we'll be off air. That's the management rule – three consecutive swear words and they shut us down ... There just remains time for me to say goodbye ... you will be hearing from me again ... I hope you won't be hearing from him again

… the anarchist … the enfant terrible spoil sport. Go on WOODCOCK! I can't stop you now … say something outrageous ...

JW: Shit.

BLT: Go on …

JW: SHIT! – Ooh, nothing, a rude word … you dirty sod, you dirty old man!

BLT: Go on you've still got a few seconds left …

JW: You fucking rotter … what a fucking rotter … he's like your Dad is he this geezer? Or your Grandad. YOU TORY FUCKER … UP THE REVOLUTION! … LONG LIVE THE WAR ON SOCIAL INEQUALITY … I STILL BELIEVE IN THE CND … SMASH THE GOVERNMENT … NEW LABOUR ARE NO BETTER THAN THE TORIES … you dirty bastard … ooh, a rude word … LONG LIVE THE MINERS! LONG LIVE THE MIGHTY REDSKINS! FREE NELSON MANDELA! SMASH THIS PUNY EXISTENCE!

Julian presses STOP on the tape recorder and takes a large swig of flat cider.

## Exercise #06: Is Julian a tragic alcoholic?

..........................................................................................................

..........................................................................................................

..........................................................................................................

..........................................................................................................

..........................................................................................................

## Quote #01: The Global Village Idiot

**"Yeah, now that I think about it, I *am* a son-of-a-bitch. Look – right there! I just insulted my own mother! Man, what an asshole I am! I deserve to die!"**

From 'The Tree of Misery', a US-based website dedicated to self-loathing.

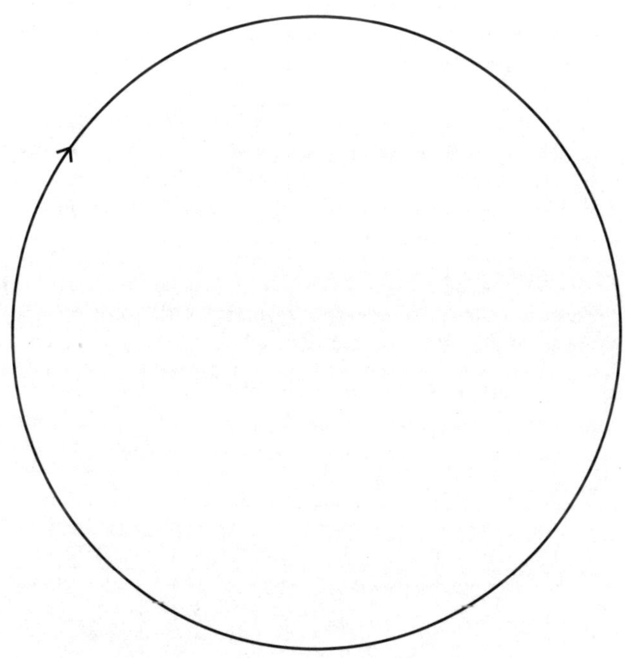

Diagram #02: A Vicious Circle

# Case Study #06: The Novelist

Jonathan Bevan lives alone. He's a part-time lecturer at the local art college. This is handy as it's only 5 minutes walk from his home. He enjoys the walk to work in the morning. Sometimes, on his way home at night Jonathan will stop off at the Barley Mow for a few hours. The Barley Mow is his escape from the pressures of work and the mundanity of the everyday. He doesn't socialise with the other lecturers, they're preoccupied with course politics, kids and mortgages; he feels that they LACK THE INITIAL IMPETUS TO MAKE ART OF ANY KIND. Jonathan doesn't really speak to the regulars at the Barley Mow either; he feels that they're pub bores who LACK THE INITIAL IMPETUS TO REALISE THEIR IDEAS. So, Jonathan drinks alone noting down the conversational oddities that will eventually form the backbone of his first novel.

On returning home Jonathan often enjoys a couple of bottles of gin. Sometimes he likes to kick his dog around for a while. Jonathan usually tries to make as much noise as possible, hoping to upset his elderly neighbours. He particularly enjoys it if they come round and start banging on his door, in his mind this legitimises the verbal and physical abuse that he inflicts on them.

**Exercise #07: Do you want to help Jonathan? If YES write out a synopsis for his first novel (including title, characters, dialogue):**

........................................................................................

........................................................................................

........................................................................................

........................................................................................

........................................................................................

........................................................................................

........................................................................................

........................................................................................

........................................................................................

........................................................................................

........................................................................................

........................................................................................

........................................................................................

........................................................................................

........................................................................................

........................................................................Thank you

## Exercise #08: Are You In Control?

Circle the percentage that you feel in control of your situation (at this moment). This will help get you into the habit of repeating this exercise at the start and end of each day. After seven days you will be able to work out your Average Personal Control for one week.

**NO CONTROL**

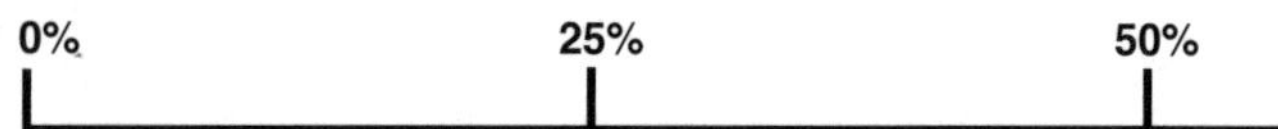

PERFECT CONTROL
75%
100%
125%

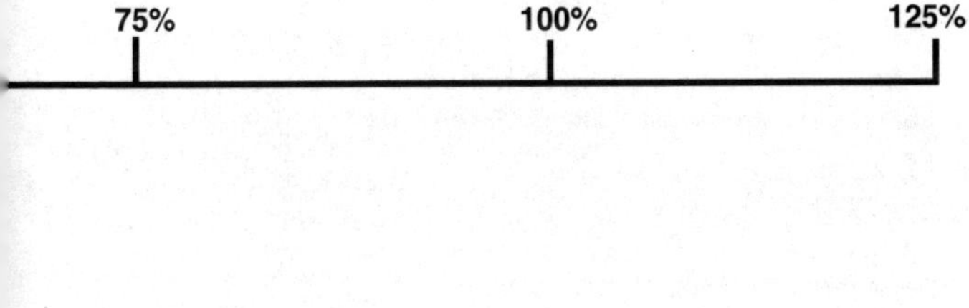

## Case Study #07: Mick The Milkman (A Bat Out Of Hell)

Mick always finished his milk round at 12.15 or thereabouts – depending on the weather and the traffic.

He'd always be in The Craic House pub before 1.00. The Craic House wasn't the nearest pub to the milk depot – but Mick didn't like to mix with the other milkmen, so he'd walk half an hour towards King's Cross, to the Craic House. He didn't mix with the locals in the pub either, but at least they didn't know him, so he didn't feel obliged to speak to them – and most importantly, they wouldn't make fun of him either.

Mick would drink  6, 7 or 8 pints by 3 o'clock – strong lager as well – straight down in near silence. At 3 o'clock he'd ring his mum from the pay phone by the toilets. Mick must have been nearly forty, but he still lived with his mum, in a flat on City Road.

Mick: Hiya Mum, it's me …
Mum:
Mick: No! … I'm not drunk. Just had a couple with Barry from …
Mum:
Mick: Oh right. Yep. OK.
Mum:
Mick: Should be back by 4.
Mum:
Mick: What's for dinner?
Mum:
Mick: Great. I love saveloy.
Mum:
Mick: And chips? Lovely. What about …
Mum:
Mick: You've been out and got beans? Oh mum, I love you.
Mum:
Mick: I can't wait.
Mum:
Mick: I love you. You know I do …

Mum:

Mick: Yes. More than anyone in the whole world. I always …

Mum:

Mick: I won't be. I'm setting off soon.

Mum:

Mick: I love you too.

Mick would then sit back on his stool at the bar. His face, always glowing red, would be flush with a purple glow. I used to think he looked like he'd just had sex. A really deep red flush, a real exhausted satisfaction. When he lit his first post-*Mum what's for dinner?* cigarette it was embarrassing – it was like a bad advert, or a scene from an ancient black and white film – the post coital cigarette metaphor.

I used to try and speak to Mick sometimes. He was always reluctant to speak to me. I think he found me too forward, too clever and arrogant maybe. I think he knew that I was laughing at him. I don't know this, but I suspect that he thought I might be trying to garner information from him – to caricature him – to use him. And sadly, he was right.

The only conversation I remember having with him was about 'favourite records'. He told me his favourite record was *Bat Out Of Hell* by Meatloaf. Without hesitation I had a vision of him in his electric milkfloat – his bloated body squeezed into his blue overalls. His fat bearded beetroot face smiling. He was singing along. His foot pressed hard on the milkfloat's accelerator. He was speeding towards a hill on the horizon. He was speeding towards the sunset. He was happy and he was free. Then, like a Bat Out Of Hell, he was gone.

**Exercise #08: Are you a Bat Out Of Hell?**..........................................

..............................................................................................................

# Case Study #08: Attempting Suicide With Erik

Erik knew nothing about English trains ... except that English trains could be relied upon to crash on a regular basis (and 'accidental death' was what he was looking for). There was no way his family and friends would ever forgive him if he took his own life. But after much research he figured out the percentages – and it seemed that he could die (seemingly) an innocent victim on an English train. Perfect. It wouldn't be his fault. He'd be a victim of circumstance and shoddy maintenance. Erik had never been to London before, but unphased he bought a daily travel card, £3.80, 'cheaper than a shotgun' he thought. All the

**Exercise #09 Imagine you are Erik. Complete A–D accordingly.**

| A. Situation | B. Your Mood |
|---|---|
| September 2002: | September 2002: |
| ...................................................... | ...................................................... |
| September 2003: | September 2003: |
| ...................................................... | ...................................................... |
| September 2004: | September 2004: |
| ...................................................... | ...................................................... |
| September 2005: | September 2005: |
| ...................................................... | ...................................................... |
| September 2006: | September 2006: |
| ...................................................... | ...................................................... |
| September 2007: | September 2007: |
| ...................................................... | ...................................................... |
| September 2008: | September 2008: |
| ...................................................... | ...................................................... |
| **Who were you with?**<br>**What were you doing?**<br>**Where were you?** | **Describe each mood in one word.**<br>**Rate intensity of mood (0–100%).** |

trains crashed on a daily basis – so it didn't matter which one he chose. I mean, he was literally going nowhere so Epping, Edgware, Elephant – what the hell? He decided to take the Circle line. Tube or train … the same thing … The End. Curtains for Erik. Not his fault – hopefully he'll be de-railed and killed within the hour. Nobody's fault. A tragic accident. That was 27 September 2002. Erik is still alive and has since entered the Guinness Book of Records as 'The Most Revolving Person In London'. To be fair to Erik, fame hasn't really changed him that much. But he's a much happier person for it.

| C. Automatic Thoughts | D. Alternative Thoughts |
|---|---|
| September 2002: | September 2002: |
| ......................................... | ......................................... |
| September 2003: | September 2003: |
| ......................................... | ......................................... |
| September 2004: | September 2004: |
| ......................................... | ......................................... |
| September 2005: | September 2005: |
| ......................................... | ......................................... |
| September 2006: | September 2006: |
| ......................................... | ......................................... |
| September 2007: | September 2007: |
| ......................................... | ......................................... |
| September 2008: | September 2008: |
| ......................................... | ......................................... |
| **What was going through my mind?**<br>**What does this say about me?**<br>**What does this mean about my future?** | **What am I afraid might happen?**<br>**What images and/or memories do I have of this situation?** |

# Case Study #09: The Last Pub (To Kill A Lion)

**Below is an account of a conversation that took place in the Anchor & Hope public house. There are several characters contributing to the conversation. With which one do you identify the most strongly? Carefully read the text (making notes below if you have to). Finally, complete the exercise that immediately follows the conversation.**

..........................................................................................

..........................................................................................

..........................................................................................

..........................................................................................

Margaret: Sandwiches are the worst thing about funerals.

Josie: Not everybody is happy with egg.

Margaret: Some people live for cheese.

Josie: I like a good volauvent at a funeral.

Margaret: Volauvents can be tricky devils.

Josie: Volauvents can be *real* bastards.

Jim: I love scones.

Alan: So do I Jim. Lovely, they are.

Dave: Scones are gay.

Jim: They aren't. I used to work on the Princess Mary making scones. They're great. You can get a mix from Tesco now. Saves all that messing about. Cuts out all the prep work. Boom. Bosh. Done. Perfect scones in no time. Just add milk and currants ... or sultanas, if you like sultanas.

Alan: Lovely. Yeah Jim. I'll give that a try. I love scones with sultanas. Just like my old mum used to make. God rest her soul.

Dave: Your mum never used to make scones.

Alan: No she didn't, you're right Dave. I forgot about that. She didn't ever make scones. She was a lovely woman though. Good as gold.
Jim: Did she use packet scone mix? Or did she make her own from flour, eggs and milk?
Alan: She didn't make scones Jim. She'd always make a lovely Sunday roast though. Lovely it was. Great big Yorkshire pudding, roast potatoes, mashed potatoes, roasted parsnips, carrots … gravy. Lovely.
Dave: It was awful, your mum's cooking.
Alan: You're right Dave. It was bloody awful.
Dave: Tasted like shit.
Alan: It tasted just like something you wouldn't feed your worst enemy.
Jim: Did she use the packet Yorkshire pudding mix or make her own from flour, eggs and milk?
Alan: I'm not sure Jim. She made her own, I think.
Dave: She used the packet stuff.
Alan: Yeah. She used the packet stuff Jim. Bloody awful, it was.
Dave: Disgusting.
Alan: Hello Roy, mate.
Roy: Hello.
Margaret: Hello Roy.
Roy: Yeah. Pint please.
Margaret: OK. How's your lovely dog?
Roy: It'd kill a Rottweiller, this dog. Big jaws, see. Bigger teeth. Stronger back. Stronger neck. More alert. Naturally more aggressive. Very powerful animal. Could pull a man's arm off.
Margaret: Oh.
Roy: He knows he's boss, see. Not insecure. Doesn't bother other dogs. Doesn't have to. Numero Uno. Top Dog. King Of The Jungle. Lord of all he surveys.
Jim: What do you feed the dog on Roy?
Roy: Steak and raw eggs.
Jim: Free range eggs?
Roy: Yeah.
Jim: Does he like milk?

## Case Study #09 (cont.)

Roy: Yeah.
Jim: Eggs and milk?
Roy: Yeah.
Jim: Does he like currants?
Roy: Yeah. Won't touch sultanas though. He despises 'em. Hates 'em.
Alan: I hate sultanas. They're disgusting.
Dave: You just said you liked 'em.
Alan: Did I Dave?
Dave: You said 'I love scones with sultanas.'
Roy: I hate 'em.
Alan: No. No. Don't get me wrong. I don't like 'em *per se*. I only like 'em in scones.
Dave: Scones are for poofs.
Jim: Watch it Dave. That's like saying I'm a poof.
Dave: Yeah.
Alan: Yeah! You are a bit of a poof, Jim! A bit of a big girl's blouse! A bit effeminate! A bit of a ladyboy!
Jim: I aren't.
Alan: No, you're right Jim. You aren't.
Dave: Could that dog kill a lion then?
Roy: Course. That's what they was bred for in Rhodesia. Lion killers ain't they? Very powerful animals.
Jim: That thing can't kill a whole lion.
Roy: Course he can. He's King Of The Jungle. Very powerful jaws.
Alan: 'Ere Roy. I'm not been funny or anything. But how do you know? ... how do you know he can kill a whole lion?
Roy: Well. When I let him off his leash in the park, right. He doesn't go up to other dogs and start barking at 'em. He doesn't go around bullying 'em, right? They come up to him. They're giving it *all that* – yap, yap, yap. But he turns the other cheek. 'Cos he knows, don't he? He just knows, see.
Dave: Know's what?
Roy: He knows that they ain't lions. So they ain't worth it.
Alan: Just think, if that dog wanted to, he could walk straight outta this pub and kill a lion.

## Exercise #10: Your Character (Complete the Following)

I think Margaret is........................................................................

I think Josie is............................................................................

I think Jim is..............................................................................

..............................................................................................

I think Dave is............................................................................

..............................................................................................

I think Alan is.............................................................................

..............................................................................................

..............................................................................................

I think Roy is.............................................................................

..............................................................................................

..............................................................................................

..............................................................................................

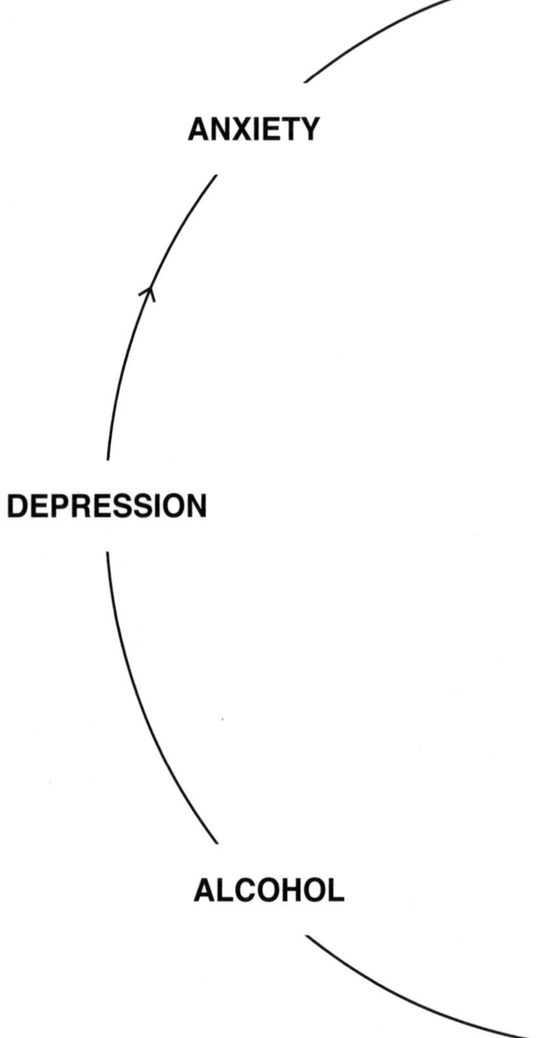
ANXIETY
DEPRESSION
ALCOHOL

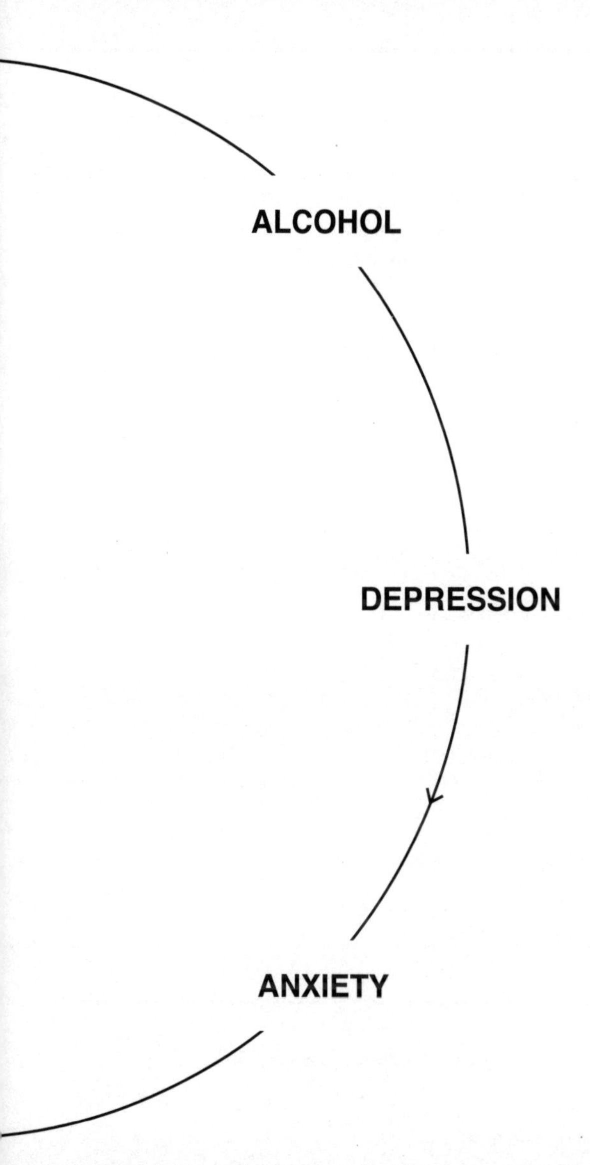

ALCOHOL
DEPRESSION
ANXIETY

# Exercise #11: Self-Humiliation (Complete A & B)

A. Absolute beliefs may remain fixed if they develop from traumatic circumstances. In order to challenge and finally overcome your 'fears', this exercise is engineered to 'self induce' personal agony. Humiliation is less powerful if it is regularly experienced. Choose a location to conduct the following experiments:

| Experiment | Location | Immediate Result |
| --- | --- | --- |
| Frequent Urination | | |
| Hysteria | | |
| Physical Violence | | |
| Paranoia | | |
| Grandiosity | | |
| Sobbing | | |
| Voluntary Vomiting | | |

B. What have I learnt from these experiments?

Frequent Urination.....................................................................................

Hysteria..................................................................................

Physical  Violence........................................................................

Paranoia................................................................................

Grandiosity..............................................................................

Sobbing................................................................................

Voluntary  Vomiting......................................................................

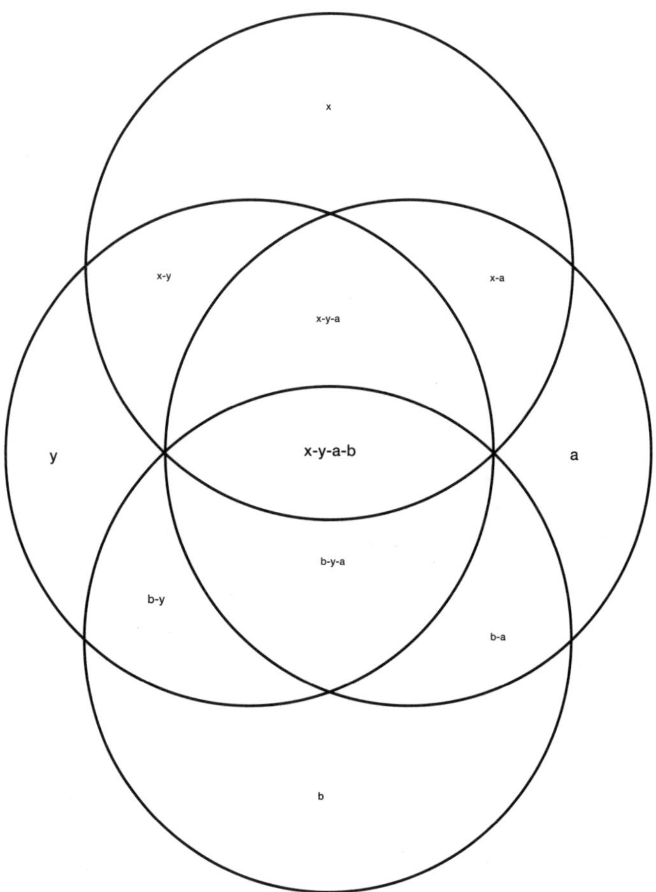
x
x-y
x-a
x-y-a
y
x-y-a-b
a
b-y-a
b-y
b-a
b

## Case Study #10: Neighbourly Aggression

Mr. Palmer: What the devil are you doing, Wilson?

Michael: Cutting my hedge.

Mr. Palmer: Cutting it? You're massacring the damn thing! Wait there, I'm need to get a witness to this. I'm going to make a citizen's arrest on you. This is a bloody disgrace.

Mr. Palmer disappears, only to return moments later with Mrs. Palmer.

Mr. Palmer: Look what the young fool has done. He's ruined the ambience of the whole street! He's mutilated his own hedge.

Mrs. Palmer: My goodness. Are you losing your mind, young man?

Michael: No. It's my hedge, and cutting it is … *like* … my only available form of *self-expression*.

Mr. Palmer: Self-expression! You bloody imbecile! I'm citizen's arresting you Wilson. Witness this Margaret, I'm arresting this man under the public order bill of …

Mrs. Palmer: What does it say? He's writing something, Andrew. He's spelling out something with his hedge … A … N … A …

Michael: It's going to spell ANARCHY, actually, Mrs. Palmer. I'm using my hedge as a symbol of protest.

## Exercise #11: Is Michael an artist? Why not?

........................................................................................

........................................................................................

........................................................................................

........................................................................................

Diagram #05: Infinite Nothingness

**Diagram #06: Nine Straight Lines

## Case Study #11: The Weatherman

'Morning.'
'Morning.'
'Funny old day today isn't it?'
'It is.'
'It's a kind of neither here nor there day isn't it? I mean it's not raining, but it's not sunny either. It's not exactly overcast, but you could hardly describe it as bright. Do you think it's windy outside? It's not that it's *not* windy, but you could hardly say it was blowing a gale. A tornado, cyclone or typhoon IT IS NOT. But similarly mill ponds, calm, tranquillity nor airless spring to mind. Would you say it was *hot* outside? *Hot* would be an exaggeration. It certainly isn't *hot*. You'd be stretched to describe it as warm even. Lukewarm would be overstepping it ... blowing it out of all proportion. But saying that, it isn't cold. To suggest it was freezing would be stupidity. But I wouldn't say it was boiling either. Neither would you say it was tropical, sweltering or roasting.'
'A pint of milk please.'
'Right you are.'
'Thank you.'
'Thank you.'

**Exercise #12: Do you cry uncontrollably without knowing why?**

....................................................................................

....................................................................................

....................................................................................

....................................................................................

....................................................................................

# Case Study #12: Everyday Life (Daily)

I was in the pub the other day. I shouldn't have been, but I was. Anyway, a woman walks in and another woman says to her – 'Hey! Shirley, you look different today.' Shirley replied 'Yeah, I've got new leggings.'

## Exercise #13: Complete the table below (for the last seven days):

| A. Day | B. Primary Activity |
|---|---|
|  |  |

# Case Study #13: The Dual Axis of Twin Evils

'I see you're smoking.'

'Yes.'

'I used to smoke … but I gave up.'

'How long since you stopped?'

'Mmm. Let me think … about three years.'

'That's good.'

'Yeah … had to pack it in. Thought I should stop when I hit forty.'

'I keep thinking that.'

'Well, you should try it. It's easier than people think. Mind you, I cut down gradually, then stopped'

'How many did you smoke a day?'

'Well … none, usually. I hate smoking, my mum used to smoke … it made the whole house stink.'

'I though you used to smoke?'

'Well I did, ocassionaly … 'til I packed it in.'

'When did you smoke?'

'Everytime I went out on the booze … couldn't stop myself … it went on for years … you know? I wouldn't have a fag, wouldn't be bothered. Then I'd go out … have a couple of pints, then BOOM! I'd be straight back on the ciggies. Every bloody time … it was like HELL! Just couldn't stop myself. A terrible thing really … used to get me down. I'd wake up in the morning, feeling awful … just bloody awful, stinking of smoke … I felt like I'd eaten a bloody ash-tray. Karen, my missus, used to go spare! She'd be like "Tony! You been smoking them fags again? Think about the kids! Think about me! Think about how we're gonna manage if you kick the bucket!" That's what made me give up really … her going on about it. Well, that was definitely one of the things … it weren't just her … I got sick of boozing as well. Boozing and smoking, terrible combination. You can't do one without the other can you? Well some people can, but I couldn't … evil stuff booze … I'm glad I stopped drinking as well … I've been so much happier since I gave it up … we all have … as a family … you know? I hated being a drinker, it was ruining my life. It was a living hell, had no power over it whatsoever.'

'How often did you go out boozing then?'

'Twice a month.'

1.
Noah drinks because he hates himself.

4.
Noah decides to go for a walk to buy some cigarettes. He then remembers that it is Saturday and that the off-licence on the corner may still be open, selling drinks illegally. It is open. Noah goes in and is served by Ramesh. Ramesh likes Noah and always tries to help him. Ramesh is reluctant to serve Noah, but Noah is insistent. Eventually, Ramesh concedes. On the way back from the off-licence Noah passes two men who have just left the local pub. Noah is sure they were staring at him. Noah shouts after the men, asking them what they were looking at. The men ignore Noah. Triumphant, Noah decides to call his estranged girlfriend using his mobile phone. This time she answers. Noah is beside himself with happiness. Noah asks his estranged girlfriend if she will marry him. She says she would have done five years ago, but he didn't want to then, so why should she now. Noah points out to his estranged girlfriend that he thinks she must be a lesbian. Noah's estranged girlfriend tells him to grow up and get a life and puts the phone down on him. Noah decides to call his estranged girlfriend back and tell her he loves her. Noah calls, nobody answers.

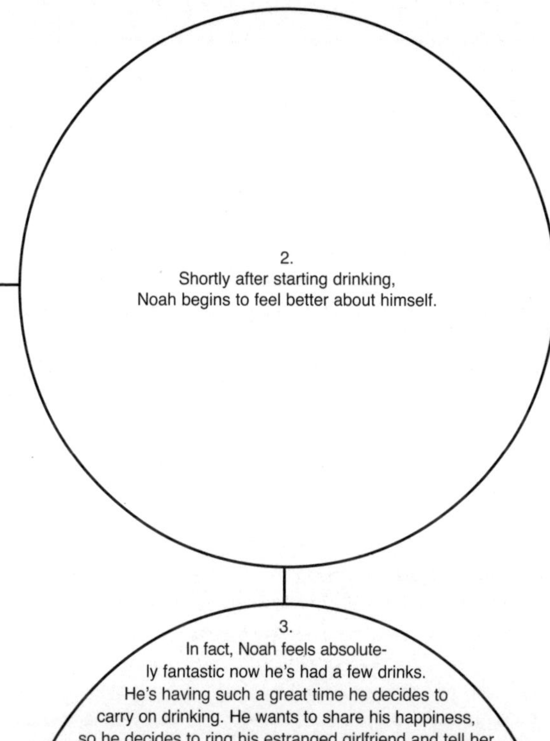

2.
Shortly after starting drinking,
Noah begins to feel better about himself.

3.
In fact, Noah feels absolute-
ly fantastic now he's had a few drinks.
He's having such a great time he decides to
carry on drinking. He wants to share his happiness,
so he decides to ring his estranged girlfriend and tell her
how much he loves her, and by the way 'will she come
back?', he's 'learnt his lesson'. Noah rings his estranged
girlfriend, her dad answers the phone. Her dad tells Noah that his
estranged girlfriend is out, and by the way, would Noah refrain from
calling after midnight. Noah explains that he had to call to ask for his
daughter's hand in marriage. Her dad explains to Noah that he is not
in a position to answer on behalf of his daughter, but given that she
left Noah over two years ago he feels it is unlikely that she will
agree to marry him. Noah then suggests that his estranged
girlfriend's father is to blame for Noah's loneliness and slams
down the receiver. Noah decides to console himself by drinking
more. He then decides to find the phone number of a girl he
met three months ago but never called. Noah locates the
phone number but is too shy to call. He decides to
call his estranged girlfriend again, because
she should be home by now. Noah
calls, nobody answers.

## Case Study #14: Oral Therapy

Therapist: So … how are we today?

Patient: Not bad thanks … well, except … I'm filled with a sense of impending doom … death … or worse: an invitation to a dinner party that I can't get out of. Why do people in London insist on inviting other people to their homes for dinner? It's a fucking conceit. To presume that someone else would like to sit in your house for hours on end talking to you about the 'relative merits of the euro' or '*your day*': 'So how was *your day* then Paul?' '*Oh, it was marvellous. First of all I woke up and wished that I hadn't. Then I remembered that I had to come here for dinner tonight and wondered if I could pretend to be ill, realising that I couldn't, I decided to have a wank. Eventually, I got out of bed. Oh! then I remembered that I had a bottle of wine left from the night before. So for about an hour or so I tried to do some work. Then I could resist the wine no longer, so I started drinking it. Then, quite drunkenly, I attempted to devise another series of increasingly elaborate excuses about why I couldn't come here. Realising I was drunk and my excuses were pathetic, I finally gave up on them and went back to bed. Then I got up and came here, smiling as I entered, you may have noticed? So here I am, excuseless, unhappy, fulfiling your desire to have me here so we can pretend that both or either of us is remotely interested in the euro.*' I have absolutely no interest in the fucking euro … why should I? It makes me sick, people just want to talk about anything don't they? They formulate opinions in order to create seemingly meaningful conversation. That's why they all read *The Guardian*. I mean … I don't believe that half these cunts who buy *The Guardian* are actually interested in it. They just feel like they HAVE to read it: in order to have something to say at their fucking dinner parties. If they didn't have to go to dinner parties they wouldn't bother reading that fucking thing. Arseholes. They live in fear of being caught out on a question about the EU or the strength of the pound in comparison to the dollar. They live their lives second hand, they formulate non-opinions in order to regurgitate them over Joanna's fucking dinner table, over Joanna's latest quiche disaster … in Joanna's Islington basement flat. I can't fucking stand them. Middle-class nobodies with their career-ettes and their sushi. If I were Prime Minister, first thing I'd do is execute them all … like Pol Pot did. Kill the liberal intelligentsia, useless bastards. I'd shoot the fucking lot of them. BANG! BANG! BANG! Class cleansing.

Therapist: *Excellent!*

## Exercise #14: Art Therapy

Use a pencil to complete the picture below. Your picture can be totally abstract or entirely realist, but it must be in response to the following statement: *The cross line is the horizon.*

## Case Study #15: Timmy's Diary

Timmy works on the roads; he has done for years. Timmy's drinking is totally out of control, yet it's as regimented as *the Changing of the Guard*.

Saturdays: Wake up 9 am go to the off-license, buy two 2-litre bottles of Olde English Cider. These are to be drunk immediately and quickly, on an empty stomach. At 10.30 am Timmy will go to The Barley Mow, less than five minutes walk from his flat (any further would've been too far). Pat the Landlady will let Timmy in through the side door and usher him into the already busy bar. Timmy'll then order a pint of Guinness with a Jack Daniels chaser. He'll drink these straight down in two gulps, using the space in between the gulps to order *the same again*. Timmy will drink five pints, with chasers, in quick succession. This, combined with his Olde English breakfast, means that within an hour of entering the pub he'll be completely smashed. Despite being virtually immobilised and more or less incapable of speech, Timmy will stay in the pub all day and night. Timmy likes to lean on the bar and strike up 'conversations' with regulars and newcomers alike. Eventually, Timmy will be so drunk that Pat'll force him out of the pub, leaving him no choice but to go home. How Timmy ever makes it home is a mystery to everyone, but he must get home because:

Sundays are the same as Saturdays.

Mondays: Timmy has to start work at 7 am every weekday. The nature of his job means that 'work' could be in Catford, Camden or even Watford. Miraculously Timmy is never late. Timmy is usually back in The Barley Mow by 6 pm. He orders his usual drinks and drinks as many of them as possible. Timmy will stay in the pub until 11.30 pm when Pat forces everyone to leave. On being asked to leave Timmy will attempt to protest to Pat. Protest is useless; Pat will simply steer Timmy's huge drunken body to the door and threaten to ban him. Timmy then leaves silently.

Tuesdays: The same as Mondays.
Wednesdays: The same as Tuesdays.
Thursdays: The same as Wednesdays.
Fridays: The same as Thursdays with the added bonus of it being Friday.

**Exercise #15: Imagine you were Timmy. Complete both columns for three situations/moods in any given week.**

| A. Situation | B. Mood |
|---|---|
| 1. | 1. |
| 2. | 2. |
| 3. | 3. |
| Who were you with?<br>What were you doing?<br>When was it?<br>Where were you? | Describe each mood in one word.<br>Rate intensity of mood (0–100%). |

# Case Study #16: The Agony (Four Times)

- Jeff works at the dry cleaners. He is a liar. Actually, to be fair he's more of a dreamer. Jeff will bore anyone and everyone with his ghost stories. Terry, the barman at the Barley Mow, likes to verify that 'Jeff has regular encounters with the spirit world' – this is Terry's favourite joke. Terry used to call Jeff 'Tales Of The Expected', for convenience he shortened this to 'T.O.T.E.', before reducing it to 'Tote', and finally 'Tit'.

- Jim is moving to Australia. He has been for four years. Jim's girlfriend Michelle is from Adelaide and she's desperate to get back there. It's extremely complicated. Jim is a trained plumber, he's self-employed, he's a decent bloke nowadays. Michelle is constantly perplexed at Jim's visa application being rejected. Jim drinks in the Barley Mow. He's been down on his luck recently: lots of jobs have fallen through, wrong parts delivered, complaints about his punctuality (even from old customers). Jim shakes and sweats and isn't moving to Australia.

- To regularly drink Strongbow cider on the King's X to Edinburgh Inter-City 125 isn't a bad thing. Sometimes, it makes the journey quicker and more fun, but other times it makes the journey more lonely, veering between giddy exuberance and claustrophopic loneliness. The reality is: trains, airports and cities can make you lonely. The supposed functionality of their structure and their utilitarian nature are not designed for personal involvement or social nicities. Pat Mosley tried to make this point to Dean Walton: shouting it through the door of the staff toilet, where Dean had locked himself in with a dozen minature bottles of spirits he'd stolen from the buffet car.

- I am on a train. I am sitting at a cramped table writing this into my laptop. The pretty girl sitting opposite me just turned to the old woman who'd recently sat down beside her and said, 'Excuse me. Do you know which way the toilets are?' The old woman replied, 'No. I'm not from round here.'

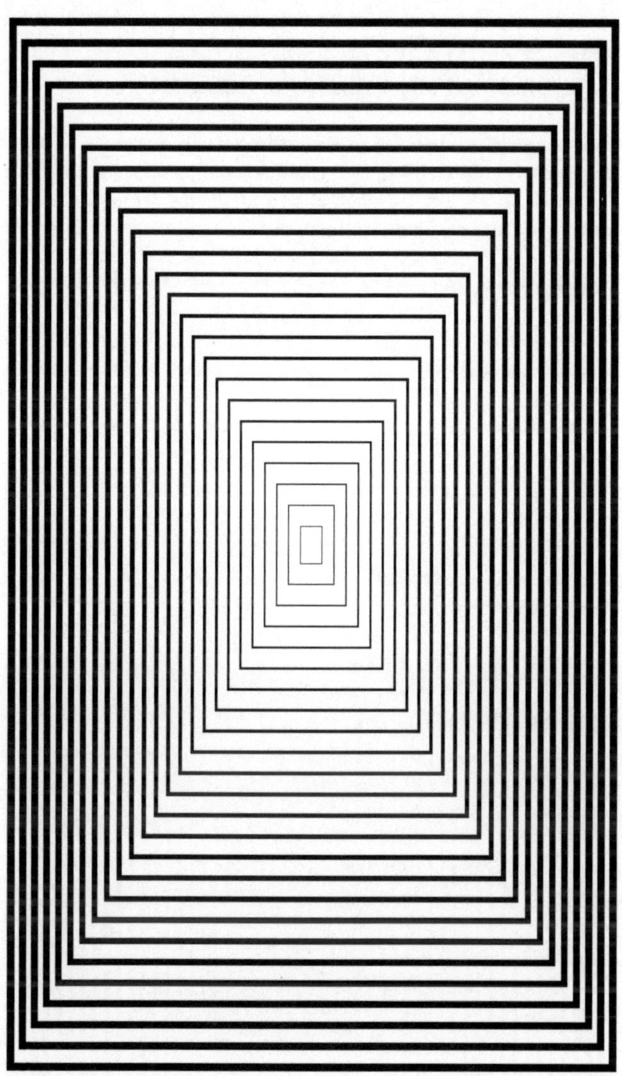

Diagram #08: A Void

## Case Study #17: How Anxiety Is Generated

**I can't remember her, but she remembers me, or seems to anyway – she could be lying. She hasn't used my name yet. I kissed her on both cheeks (of course) and attempted to instigate the vaguest of friendly conversations.**

**I haven't seen you for ages …**
I hope.

**How's it going?**
This is good because it gives her a chance to mention what she does and who she does it with, and if I recognise the name of one of the people she does whatever she does with, that could be the key to remembering who she is, then I might tentatively and reluctantly test out her name.

**What are you working on?**
This is also good – because it's extremely non-specific and allows her to explain if she's an artist or a curator, I know she's one or the other, everybody is.

**Oh great, he's fantastic, yes.**
Now she's telling me about an artist that I've never heard of. I put this down to my own ignorance. Judging by her excitement, he must be quite famous.

**Hi, how's it going? … Ah yes.**
Bollocks. Now she's introducing me to her mate. He says we've met.

**Yes. That *was* hilarious.**
Now he's telling me that we had a 'mad' night out once. I've never seen him before in my fucking life, I'm sure.

**Ah yes … Hi, how's it going?**
Fucking hell. Now there's three of them.

**I saw Nicky last night.**

That went down like a lead balloon. I thought they must be his mates. They're obviously not. Who are they?

Oh arseholes. Now Tess is coming over and I'll have to introduce her. Shit. I've got to move away quick. I've got to put as much space between me and them as possible. I'll have to make a run for it.

**I'm just going to get another drink. Does anybody else want one?**

Why did I ask them if they want a fucking drink? Now, they all want one. Now I'll have to come back.

Oh fucking rat's cocks. Now Tess is here.

**This is Tess ... everyone.**

I hope 'everyone' will suffice in this context. I should at least try the first girl's name out. No. No I shouldn't, it's not worth it. I might be friends with her.

**Exercise #16: What would you do next? Explain how and why:**

......................................................................................

......................................................................................

......................................................................................

## Exercise #17: Complete the following:

1. I am.......................................................................................................

...............................................................................................................

...............................................................................................................

...............................................................................................................

...............................................................................................................

...............................................................................................................

...............................................................................................................

...............................................................................................................

...............................................................................................................

...............................................................................................................

2. Others are.............................................................................................

3. The world is ........................................................................................

## Case Study #18: Two Johns (And One Alan)

I met an old bloke in a pub today. He proudly announced to me, 'I'm John and I'm a schizophrenic.' Then he sat down at my table and pointed behind my shoulder to another, slightly younger man standing alone next to the fruit machine. 'See him there? He's my friend Alan ... he's a schizophrenic as well.' It did occur to me that at this point most people would've made their excuses and left. John then started a one way conversation: 'This is my local pub. I always come here ... or go somewhere else. I sometimes go to the Anchor ... when I'm not coming in here. I suppose you could say I was born round here ... though I was *actually* born in Reading. I was born in a hospital that was *in fact* a really a big manor house ... it's just by the train station. Do you know it? ... it's not there any more. December 18th 1938  I was born ... I don't work in the music industry, though most people think I do ... because I have a beard. Have you ever been to Amsterdam? I went there last year. Off my head I was ... I walked from Amsterdam train station to Utrecht train station ... twenty-five miles that is ... I didn't mean to, I was just trying to find a pub that'd serve me ... but none of them would ... so I just got the train back to Amsterdam from Utrecht and went to stay at my friend Alice's house. She's a schizophrenic as well.'

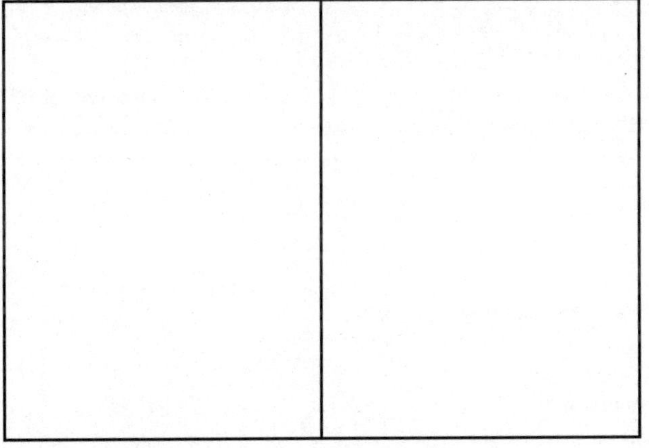

**Diagram #10: Two Johns**

## Case Study #19: Julian (A Slight Reprise)

Julian arrived slightly early at Alan Jeffreys' house. Alan lived on Cambridge Avenue in Goole. Cambridge Avenue was a nice street of 1950s bungalows and small villas – all with immaculate front gardens and neatly trimmed privet hedges. Alan worked from home as a hypnotherapist, so it was easy to catch him there. Alan had remembered in an instant who Julian was when he'd e-mailed; despite the fact that they'd barely spoken all the way through school.

'Mr. Jeffreys, I presume.'
'Julian – Hi – please come in.'

Julian was wearing his 'Kurt Cobain 1967–1994' T-shirt with torn Levi's jeans, he was carrying his rucksack and camera tripod.

'Come through to the office.'

Julian followed Alan into a small backroom. The room was surprisingly dark, with fine coloured linen draped from the walls: kind of Morroccan, or like a harem. On every shelf there were tiny ornaments from the Far East: Buddhas and religious icons. There were framed pictures too; Julian took these to be Alan's wife and twin daughters (he'd read about them on Friend's Reunited).

'Have a seat Julian.' Alan pointed at a nasty brown plastic office chair sitting opposite his almost empty desk. Julian sat down, resting his rucksack and tripod beside him. Alan sat down behind the desk and shuffled his yellowed computer keyboard to one side.

'Tea?'
'Cool. Earl Grey.'
'Only herbal I'm afraid. Ginseng?'
'No … I'll pass.'
'Mind if I do?'
'Not at all.'
'I don't have beer.'
'I'm cool.'

Alan stood up and took three paces across the room to the kettle. It stood on a stained white plastic tray. He shook the kettle, switched it on, then dropped a tea bag into an ethnic looking terracotta mug.

Julian studied Alan as he waited for the kettle to boil. Alan had changed since school … kind of. Julian only remembered him in school uniform: grey slacks, navy blue blazer, navy blue sweater, white shirt, navy blue and gold striped tie. Alan was one of the few who insisted on wearing school uniform, despite the fact that it wasn't compulsory. He was one of those people who you'd imagine probably wore his uniform on weekends too.

Alan was dressed in a flowing white cheesecloth blouson. His greasy hair was really long, almost to the middle of his back and held in place by what seemed to be half a brown leather purse with a prototype of a pencil shoved through it. He still had his glasses, exactly the same rectangular gold rimmed ones he'd had at school. He had awful jeans too Julian noticed: sort of snow-washed drainpipes, definitely not Levi's.

'So … Alan … you've changed.'
'Yeah … I guess.'
'At least you've got rid of the acne.'
'Yeah … some time ago now.'

Julian remembered why he'd always hated Alan. Alan was parochial.

'So Julian … what about you? You're living in London?'
'Yeah. Been down there nearly twenty years. It's home now, I suppose.'
'It must be great. Isn't it? I used to go there sometimes … when I worked at the Vauxhall garage.'
'You were a mechanic?'
'God no! I worked on the computers … after they took me off sales. But that's what I went there as … a car salesman. I was really good at it … well, kind of. I loved doing it. Still, they moved me to computers.'
'Really?' Julian tried to picture Alan selling cars.

# Case Study #19: Julian (A Slight Reprise) – (cont.)

Alan sat back down at his desk, the steaming Ginseng tea in front of him.

'So … what do I need to do … for this film?'
'It's simple really,' Julian said as he set up the tripod and screwed the camera
on to it. 'I'm going to ask you a few questions. You just need to answer them
… as honestly as possible.'

'Sounds easy enough.' Alan smiled.

Julian adjusted the tripod and camera until he was happy that it was exactly at
Alan's head height: his head filling the whole frame. Then he reached into his
rucksack and pulled out a large arc light with a fitted stand (it was similar to
a standard desktop lamp, but the bulb was three or four times larger). He
placed the lamp on Alan's desk and angled it to his face. He plugged it in but
didn't turn it on.

'Almost ready … yeah, it's really straightforward – I think it'll only last five
or ten minutes at the most, depends really.'

'Great … erm … what are the questions about?'

Julian flicked the light on; it illuminated the darkened room like a Battle of
Britain searchlight – it almost blinded Alan – who shielded his eyes.

'YOU! The questions are about you. Your youth, your life now …'
'Julian. Please. That's too bright, it's hurting my eyes.'
'Don't look at it directly … you'll be fine, as I say … this won't take long.'
'Ok.' Alan tried to make himself comfortable. Magnified through the camera
lens, his pock marked skin resembled the surface of the moon.
'And … ACTION!' Julian flicked on the camera.
'NAME?'
'Alan Jeffreys.'
'FULL NAME.'
'Alan Keith Jeffreys.'

'DO YOU REMEMBER ME?'
'Yes.'
'WHO AM I?'
'Julian Woodcock.'
'HOW DO YOU KNOW ME?'
'I was in your class … at school.'
'DO YOU REMEMBER WHAT YOU WERE FAMOUS FOR AT
SCHOOL?'
'Erm … no.'
'YOU HAD THE BIGGEST PORN COLLECTION EVER ASSEMBLED
IN GOOLE.'
'Julian please … this is …'
'TRUE OR FALSE?'
'Well … maybe … I don't know.'
'ADMIT IT.'
'Ok … maybe I did.'
'SAY IT. STATING YOUR FULL NAME – NAME FIRST'
'My name is Alan Keith Jeffreys. I had the biggest porn collection ever
assembled in Goole.'
'WHAT DO YOU DO NOW?'
'Hypnotherapy.'
'SPECIALISING IN WHAT?'
'Well … natural child birthing.'
'And … CUT!' Julian stopped the camera and flicked the light off, 'IT'S A
WRAP! That's it. Thanks Alan … you were great!' Julian lit a cigarette and
sat back down on the plastic chair.
'That's it?'
'Yep.' Julian started to pack away the camera into his bag.
'But … I thought this was going to be a history of us?'
'Well it is … it's about lots of things … it's about Goole, it's about destiny
… it's about us … *it's about me*. Don't worry Alan … You'll get a good
eight or nine seconds screen time.'
'Is that all?'
'FUCKING HELL ALAN! SOME PEOPLE WON'T EVEN BE  IN IT.'

# Exercise #18: What *is* actually wrong with you?

Text & Design: Scott King

Editorial Coordination: Lionel Bovier
Editing and Proofreading: Clare Manchester
Print: Musumeci S.p.A., Quart





Printed in Europe.

Published by:
JRP|Ringier
Limmatstrasse 270, CH–8005 Zurich
Tel. +41 (0) 43 311 27 50
Fax +41 (0) 43 311 27 51
www.jrp-ringier.com
info@jrp-ringier.com

ISBN 978-3-905829-95-2

For a list of our partner bookshops
or for any general questions, please contact
JRP|Ringier directly at info@jrp-ringier.com,
or visit our homepage www.jrp-ringier.com
for further information about our program.

JRP|Ringier books are available international-
ly at selected bookstores and from the following distribution partners:

Switzerland:
AVA Verlagsauslieferung AG, Centralweg 16,
CH–8910 Affoltern a.A.,
verlagsservice@ava.ch, www.ava.ch

Germany and Austria:
Vice Versa Distribution GmbH,
Immanuelkirchstrasse 12, D–10405 Berlin,
info@vice-versa-distribution.com,
www.vice-versa-distribution.com

France:
Les presses du réel, 35 rue Colson, F–21000
Dijon, info@lespressesdureel.com,
www.lespressesdureel.com

UK and other European countries:
Cornerhouse Publications, HOME, 2 Tony
Wilson Place, UK–Manchester M15 4FN,
publications@cornerhouse.org,
www.cornerhousepublications.org/books

USA, Canada, Asia, and Australia:
ARTBOOK|D.A.P., 155 Sixth Avenue,
2nd Floor, USA–New York, NY 10013,
orders@dapinc.com, www.artbook.com

In the same series:

David Robbins
*Ice Cream Social*
ISBN 978-2-940271-55-9

Francis Baudevin
*Hello Spiral!*
ISBN 978-3-905829-69-3